The Intrusive Thoughts of The Lioness

Tamara Pryor

BookLeaf Publishing

India | USA | UK

Presentation by *BookLeaf Publishing*

Web: www.bookleafpub.com

E-mail: info@bookleafpub.com

ISBN: 9789360944957

First edition 2024

God gets the Glory!

*To my Mom, thanks for loving and
supporting ME!*

*R.I.P. to my Pops, daughter, and all my
deceased loved ones who helped to inspire
ME!*

*To my babies Heaven, Harmonie, Hakeem,
and Hassan thanks for Loving ME!*

To all my family and friends near and far

Tam Tam Thanks and Love Y'all TOO

And Thanks for supporting ME!

ACKNOWLEDGEMENT

I would like to thank and acknowledge my Queen, my Mom, my DEBO for giving me life and for all your support and love in all I do, the good and the bad you were there and I'm thankful….

To my Daddy my "Pops" (may you R.I.P) even from the Heavenly skies, you looking out like always, you are truly missed.

To My H crew…y'all who I do it for ALWAYS…mom loves you all….

Big acknowledgement to my Baby sister Danielle for the inspiration to do this challenge…

To the Big Sis Shonna, thanks for being a creative inspiration…

To all my family and friends that have played major parts in my life which ultimately led to my writings....YOU KNOW WHO YOU ARE!! Thanks for allowing me the time and space to complete this challenge.

To the BookLeaf Publishing Team that have put up with me through this process I truly am grateful for you all.

Heavenly Father GOD thank you for continuing to breathe life into me when so many times I wanted to give up, you weren't done with me YET!

PREFACE

My thoughts and feelings on paper
Intertwined with rhythm and rhyme
This is a book of my poems
It's about TIME!!

ME!

Often failing to love ME!
Not understanding why I don't like ME!
Often putting EVERYTHING before ME!
Bipolar about ME!
Sometimes caring what others think of ME!
Other times not giving a FUCK
Because I'm going to be ME !
But WHO IS ME?
BIG ME!
Li'l ME!
FAT ME!
Thick ME!
Old ME!
New Me!
Happy ME!
Sad ME!
No matter the ME!
I'm free to be ME!

My Li'l Journey

Life started off the fairway
Remembering often times hitting the highway
Family trips and reunions was our thang
Meeting up with cousins to talk the country
slang
Later on ended up in University Park
For me that's when life began to be dark
At times feeling alone because now I have a
broken home
Feeling like all I knew is somehow now gone
Not adapting well to the change
Allowing my anger to control the pain
On to a new home we ended up on Lisa Lane
Trying to be open to my new norm I have to
maintain
The hell I then put my mother through
Is payback x10 this I know is true
Facing many challenges along the way
Thanking God I've even made it to this day
Adventuring off thinking I was grown
Moving to Nashville to call it my new home
leaving all the help I knew behind
with a great plan in mind
But LIFE and MOTHERHOOD took a turn for
the worse

I've now given up my daughter and seeing my
daddy in a hearse
GRIEVING with guilt took control of me
Blinding me from the other abuse I didn't see
Homeless with 3 kids is where I ended up
But hey I'm The Lioness, I'll never give up
Hustled and sacrifice for places to stay
But having the faith that God will make a way
Moving in our place on my dad's death date
Made it all real to me that this was fate
The move still came with struggles I caused on
myself
Knowing somethings I brought I should have
left.

Family Love

Holidays and Birthdays
are celebrated together
Throwing a Bar-B-Que
just because of good weather
calls and text just to check in
Hey, what's up, how you been
Pull up game used to be strong
But over the years
the bond has gone.
Family feuds causing more distance
than the miles.
hoping one day to be greeted again with smiles.
It's okay to agree to disagree but don't stay there
and just let it be.
Allow the love to conquer all
because a family that prays together
stays together and we shall not fall.
Remembering GOD loves us all

To Mom!

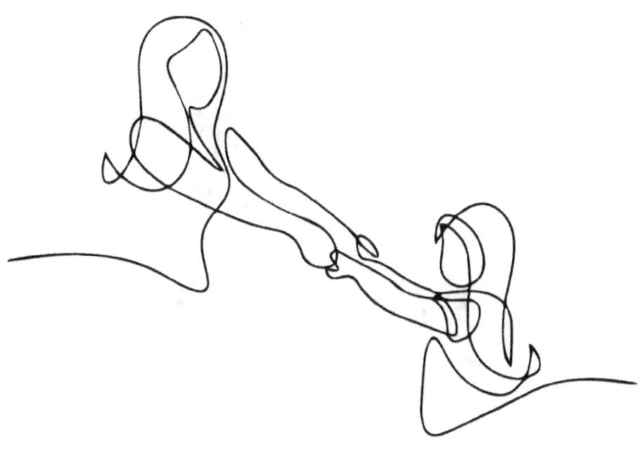

I'm the baddest of us all
but she likes me the most
Never missing a call
On my Queen I will boast
I put her through a lot of hell
But her love for me never failed
Doing what she needed to do
to make sure I didn't go to jail
I don't think I say it enough
How much you mean to me
I've made this life of mine rough
But you continued to pray for me
I guess "it's the God in me" you see
But whatever it is
Thanks for loving ME

Daddy

What am I to do
Now that you are gone
But I know you good
you're going to your heavenly home
What a man, Heaven is about to receive
I know this in my heart
because you believed
I wanted so bad for you to stay
But it's OK
I'll see you again another day
words can't express the way I feel
but knowing it's really real
you gave your all
even to a stranger
you did all you could do to keep us out of danger
You are now in no more pain

your legs you have regain
Go find Grandma and baby Angel too
They will give you a tour all the way through
Grab your fishing pole and load your bus
You can now redo all you did with us
who am I to question the Master's plan
Heaven is about to gain an awesome man

A Letter to Dad

7 years you've been gone
I'm still trying to figure out
where I went wrong
People say I'm not to blame
but knowing I left
makes me feel ashamed
I'm missing you like crazy
Always feeling numb inside
Smoking my life away and being lazy
but it's the only place to hide
DADDY I WANT YOU BACK
But I know it's selfish of me to feel this way
So I'll just pray for a better day
But, I didn't get the chance to say goodbye
I guess you didn't want to see me cry
Life has been rough without you

And oh I've messed up bad too
I don't know where life is leading me right now
But I've gotta get through someway somehow

Love Always, Daddy's Girl TamTam

Sister Sista

Some are biological
born with the same blood
Learning together
how to get it out the mud

Some are from the hood
them are the Ridas
"That wish a Nigga would"
Because we're soul survivors

Some we beef with during our years at school
But through the years of growth we became cool

Some we met at work
that started out as a jerk

Some we met at church
all there for a word
and on a search

So no matter the meet and greet
We all have the same father
that we must strive to meet

So Daddy said to Love

Because He is Love
and if we all stick together
we will make it to our home above

So acknowledge a sista
on your daily walk
Don't be scared to start a convo
and just talk

Hey Sis
Yeah you boo
I pray God's favor over you

I'm the Momma

Motherhood came by the way of a surprise
Outside being wild
I was living a disguise
Following a trend
and doing what others do
I ended up with kids not 1 but 2
Determined to be the best mom I could be
Here I am on the way with child #3
Guess God knew I needed my own personal
Angel of Hope
But to be honest her death almost had me on
dope
Grieving wrong
my head was gone
knowing she wasn't there
feeling like that was unfair

So to the streets I go
Now pregnant with baby #4
Aborting was never an option for me
Knowing I could never live mentally free
So I ended up with 5
and only 4 still are alive
and I do what I can to make sure we survive
Mothering didn't come with no book
so some of my mistakes are left off the hook
allowing another chance to take a look
on how to do things right
because mothering is a daily fight

Happy Mother's Day

Day by day
We make a way
Telling ourselves
We gonna be OK
Hiding the hurt and pain
Not allowing those memories to remain
Many of us do it on our own
Letting God fill the gap of us feeling alone
We struggle we strive
We know how to survive
and by His Grace we are still alive
Pat yourself on the back
For picking up these daddies slack
Be proud because we're still standing tall
And if we stick together we will never fall
And remember TamTam loves you ALL!

International Women's Day

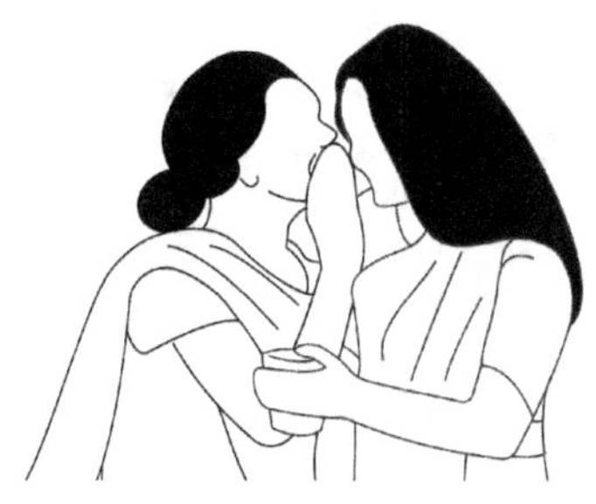

Hey Women of the World
Some young and some old
Living in a world that feels so cold
some facing this world alone
Enduring till the end
Until all hope is gone
we come in all shapes and sizes
going through the days with silent cries
facing society's do's and don't's
bussing our ass for our needs and wants
some loaning for the love of a man
but nowadays we can't even ask them for a hand
Some raising boys to men on our own
all the while the daddy too scared to pick up the
phone
Being called bitter for asking for support
But all we needed was time

that would have kept us out of court
Birthing the future with boys and girls
So yes it's true when they say we run the world
So thanks for acknowledging how we have
paved the way
It took a fight just to get this day
Happy International Women's Day

Every Day is Mother's Day

Happy Mother's Day right
But please understand
it's Mother's Day every day and every night
There is no limit, there is always a fight
thank you for giving us this one day
But hold up buddy because I got a lot to say
we may bend but we don't break
it's all because of the Lord's sake
mothering didn't come with no book
but I'm going to be honest
some of y'all sorry and got it easy and off the
hook
But for the ones that are there
there's no limit to what we will bare
2 to 3 jobs just to make sure you eat
and make sure you got shoes on your feet
but oh no not just some shoes
you want the J's
so here it is we make a way
My bad choice left you fatherless
so yes I struggle to make you worry less
I miss out on time I would love to spend with
you

but I'm at work boo and I'm the only one feeding
you
Do I feel entitled oh but hell yes I do
that's Ok because I still thank God for you
If you still have your mother
please treat her right
and know that everyday she wakes
you are the reason she fights
Happy Mother's Day

Happy Father's Day

Who's my daddy
Where's my daddy
Are the questions I get from my child
is knowing really worth their wild
Holidays and birthdays don't even matter to
them
For all he knows is he really the father of him
No money to give
no time to spend
they rather kick it with their homies
or do time in the pin
But you want me to wish you a Happy Father's
day
Happy Father's day to who
nigga please
Happy Father's day to me
the one who puts clothes on their back
shoes on their feet
and give them food to eat
The one that always makes time
the one with no option
I got to give up my last dime
but I don't mind
Niggas grow up and get like me
they think they are strong

but really they are WEAK
they couldn't begin to do what I do
not even a little peek
I love me cause I've got my own
no it's not another sad love song
the kids are the ones left alone
but don't you worry mom's got your back
We have been doing it for years picking up your
daddy's slack...
Because y'all niggas are really wack.

Sad Dad

It's sad
these kids are
left with no dad
by the choice of a boy
who rather plays with a toy
no way you can call yourself a man
when you chose the wrong option
and ran
Boy please when you say the child should call
the father
you ain't doing nothing no way why even bother
Money can't buy love
So don't make loving your child this hard for
you
Just pick up the phone they would love to hear
from you too
But you make excuses for not even a call

So please don't tell them you tried your all
Y'all be mad about child support
but understand when you leave
we are the support
Now I'm left to see you only in court
More excuses are yet to be made
Now I bet you wish you had paid

M.A.D.D. (Mother Against Deadbeat Dads)

Yeah I'm MADD
been mad
and you've been sad
because you don't know
how to be a dad
crying on the phone
saying my son should call
Boy please he doesn't know you at ALL
Denying my son like you were something to
claim
But, unfortunately you're the only one to blame
Accountability, yes I'll take
but I'll never say my son was a mistake
you didn't get your momma that paternity test
when all of this could have been laid to rest
so that sent me on another quest
To the YT people I go
to file these papers
just to let you know
that I'm not the one you should have played
But you've been doing this for so long
guess you thought you had it made
this ain't never been about money
I been knew you were broke

It's the principle of the matter
now you're about to have a stroke
Depressed you say
Do I suppose to care
Boy you know how you did my son wasn't fair
So go ahead and do your time
Because I have always told you
whether it be your time or dime
you will pay for mine
Signed a bitter baby momma of a son
Unfortunately when you are locked up
still no one has won

Letter to Grandma

There were many things I wanted to say
But I tried to wait for that perfect day
But now that God has called you home
I'll have to say it in this poem
thanks for being the best Grandma you could be
thanks for always believing in me
You soared as a wife and mother
I know my mom, aunts and uncle
wouldn't have had another
Sorry I didn't get a chance to say goodbye
But it brings comfort in knowing you are in the
Heaven's sky
Knowing you are safe, happy and free from pain
Those wings you have surely gained
For this journey that we all must take
and each must go alone
It's all in the master's plan

A step on the road to our final home
We will miss you now that you are gone
You are in a better place now
and you are not alone
Say Hi to Grandpa, auntie Pat and auntie
Annie-Lee
Say Hi to Grandma Jewell and give my Angel a
hug from me

I love you, Grandma

Angel of Trinity Faith

I called up to Heaven and told Angel to come to
the gate
She asked, "But, Mom why?"
I told her to come and welcome her new
playmate
She said, "Mom, who is it?"
I said, "It's your cousin Trinity Faith."
This was all a part of the Master's Plan so don't
be late
Angel said, Mom, I'm so excited, I have so much
to show her
I'll welcome her with a big loud cheer
I know she will love it up here
Mom, don't be sad, I know she will be missed
I will welcome her with open arms and a big ole
Kiss
She's in a better place, this I know you know
You had your time so let her go
We will play together, laugh, sing, and dance
Remember, Mom, God had these plans in
advance
We will walk around Heaven all day
Singing together a happy song
Don't think that she will be alone
I have a lot of people to go and phone

to tell of the new Angel that's to arrive
to you she's gone but to us she's alive
Be happy for her she's in no more pain
Miss Trinity is an Angel we have gain
I'll go get her grandma Christin to be by my side
So Trinity will feel welcomed coming to the
other side

Unc Ray

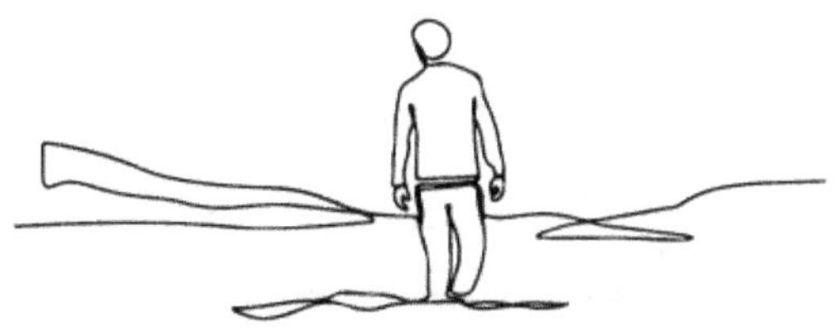

How do I say goodbye to my uncle Ray
Wishing to God I had one more day
Finding it hard to believe that you are gone
Never again being able to reach you by phone
Not even distance separated our love
But now you are an angel in the sky above
What a Merry Christmas it was for dad
Greeting you at the gates surely made him glad
You always kept it real
with one of your favorite sayings "What's the
deal?"
There will never be another
Oh so smooth
You are my definition of cool

R.I.P. George Floyd

You kneeled on his neck for 9.29
When this little crime
could have ended with a fine
What was really on your mind
He begged you for help
He screamed in pain
You literally took this man's life in vain
You made this personal
when you didn't follow the commands
Of that badge that you wear
as you held down his hands
Was it the color of his skin
that caused so much hate from within
show me you're human
and explain to me why

You wanna win this case
Take the stand and try not to lie
MURDERER YOU ARE
GUILTY YOU SHALL BE
AND IF NOT
HELL IS WHAT THIS WORLD WILL SEE

Who Cares

I care too much
Something I often do
Believing what you said
Was always true!
Falling fast!
Always get me in trouble
Never preparing my heart
For the royal rumble
So NOW here we are beat up again
Back to repair mode I go
Lying to myself AGAIN
Always promising to take things slow
Never allowing my heart to heal
Taking a mental note that heartbreak is real
Has it truly ever healed!

What is This

I don't want this to end
Here I go falling weak again
It probably won't ever be the same
I've kinda picked up on your game
So I'll play alone
possible do some overtime
until the love is gone
or until you're finally mine
But we know that will never be
Those li'l visits don't do enough for me
traveling miles just for some dick
for a nigga that can't even call when he's sick
But I won't trip I allowed it to be this way
So I'll just wait for that text another day

Long Distance

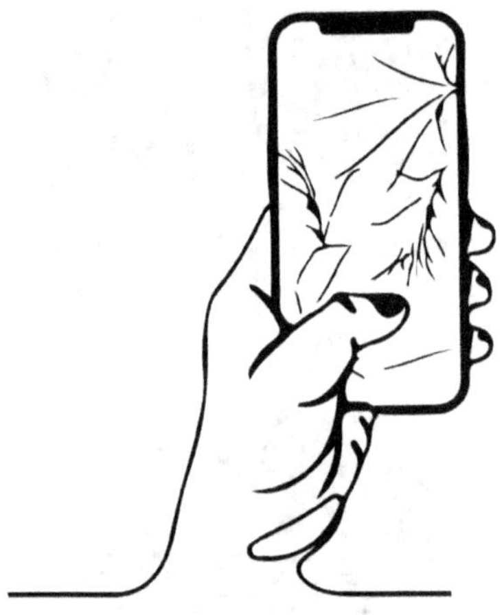

You go ghost without saying bye
and not even having a why
I thought the bond was better than that
But I guess not so I'm left to react
fighting the urge not to text yo ass
knowing that I should just leave you in the past
Why I'm acting like this, something new
You always left me hanging on view
I'll fight my heart and leave it as be
them 600 miles kept you safe from me
taking another hit on my heart for not loving me
mad at the decisions I make
How much more will I take
Seriously tired of the constant heartbreak

Friends w/Benefits

Friends with benefits
What does that look like to me
Friends with benefits
Are you able to call or text me
Friends with benefits
Are we allowed to take walks in the park
Friends with benefits
Or are we only able to see each other when it's
dark
Friends with benefits
Can I care how you feel
Friends with benefits
Or is that doing too much I need to chill
Friends with benefits
What does it look like to you
Friends with benefits
Are you required to stay true
Friends with benefits
How long do the benefits last
Friends with benefits
Do we just become lovers and friends from the
past
Friends with benefits
What happens if one falls in love
Friends with benefits

Can you be sent from above
Friends with benefits
Can be confusing I see
Friends with benefits
When the only benefit is ME!

Fling

So what we gonna do is be grown about this shit
Cause we gotta make sure this is gonna be a
good fit
So let's be honest up front
that way we don't have to stunt
we're gonna call a thing a thing
So if I'm just a fling
Let me know
so I'll know how to swing
I accept bullshit better when I ain't gotta figure it
out
Y'all niggas out here breaking hearts just for
clout
So be careful how you treat me when playing
with my heart
Things can get ugly when I fall apart

21 Days

Procrastination I wear it well
this 21 days I put myself through Hell
never taking the time to just sit down and write
so yeah I decided to procrastinate all through the
night
21 poems is all I needed to do
So I focused on the old instead of the new
challenging myself to complete this all the way
through
Hoping this challenge will really be a dream
come true

The Lioness

The other side of me
is the Lioness you see
Fierce is her walk
passionate when she talks
Aggressively loving and oh so bold
Fighting in a world that's oh so cold
But she doesn't stop
She has a heart of gold
Her strength is rooted in gentleness
Allowing her Pride
to never show her as helplessness
Often being judged
always being told she's mean
She just straightened her Crown
Because she still reigns as Queen